GRAPHIC HISTORY

THE CREATION OF THE
U.S. CONSTITUTION

by Michael Burgan
illustrated by Gordon Purcell and
Terry Beatty

Consultant:
Philip Bigler, Director
The James Madison Center
James Madison University
Harrisonburg, Virginia

Capstone
press

North Mankato, Minnesota

Graphic Library is published by Capstone Press,
1710 Roe Crest Drive, North Mankato, Minnesota 56003.
www.capstonepub.com

Library of Congress Cataloging-in-Publication Data
Burgan, Michael.
The creation of the U.S. Constitution / by Michael Burgan; illustrated by Gordon Purcell and Terry Beatty.
p. cm.—(Graphic library. Graphic history)
Includes bibliographical references and index.
ISBN-13: 978-0-7368-6491-6 (hardcover) ISBN-10: 0-7368-6491-1 (hardcover)
ISBN-13: 978-0-7368-9653-5 (softcover pbk.) ISBN-10: 0-7368-9653-8 (softcover pbk.)
1. United States. Constitution—Juvenile literature. 2. United States—Politics and government—1775–1783—Juvenile literature. 3. United States—Politics and government—1783–1789—Juvenile literature. 4. Constitutional history—United States—Juvenile literature. I. Purcell, Gordon, ill. II. Beatty, Terry, ill. III. Title. IV. Series.
E303.B88 2007
342.7302'9—dc22 2006004078

Summary: In graphic novel format, tells the story of the debates, disagreements, and compromises that led to the formation of the U.S. Constitution during the Constitutional Convention of 1787.

Art Director
Bob Lentz

Designers
Jason Knudson and Bob Lentz

Colorist
Melissa Kaercher

Editor
Christine Peterson

Editor's note: Direct quotations from primary sources are indicated by a yellow background.

Direct quotations appear on the following pages:

Page 4, from *The Works of Benjamin Franklin*, edited by Jared Sparks (Boston: Hillard, Gray, and Company, 1840).

Pages 19, 25 (center and left), from the U.S. Constitution at the National Archives in Washington, D.C. (http://www.archives.gov/national-archives-experience/charters constitution_transcrip.html).

Page 21, from the adoption of the U.S. Constitution by the state of Massachusetts as recorded in Elliot's Debates (http://memory.loc.gov/ammem/amlaw/lwed.html).

Page 25 (bottom right), quote attributed to George Washington as documented by the Library of Congress (http://memory.loc.gov/ammem/pihtml/pinotable.html).

Printed in the United States 5889

Table of Contents

CHAPTER 1

GOVERNMENT FOR THE REVOLUTION

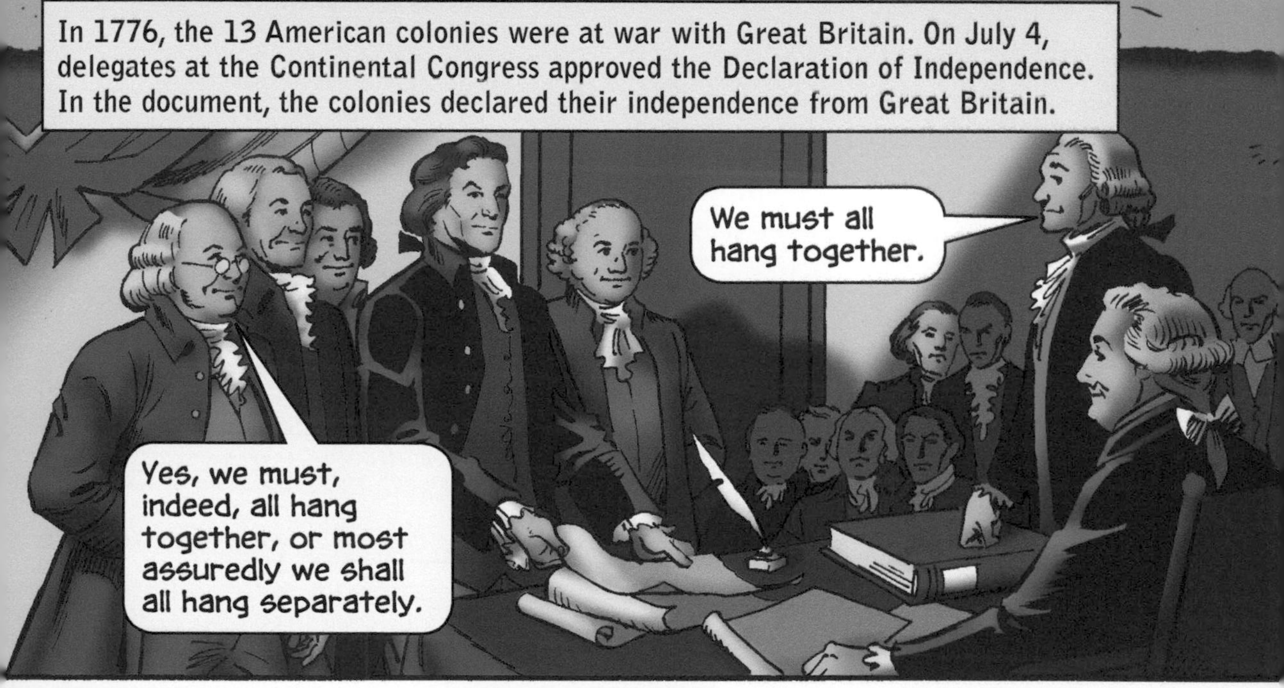
In 1776, the 13 American colonies were at war with Great Britain. On July 4, delegates at the Continental Congress approved the Declaration of Independence. In the document, the colonies declared their independence from Great Britain.
We must all hang together.
Yes, we must, indeed, all hang together, or most assuredly we shall all hang separately.

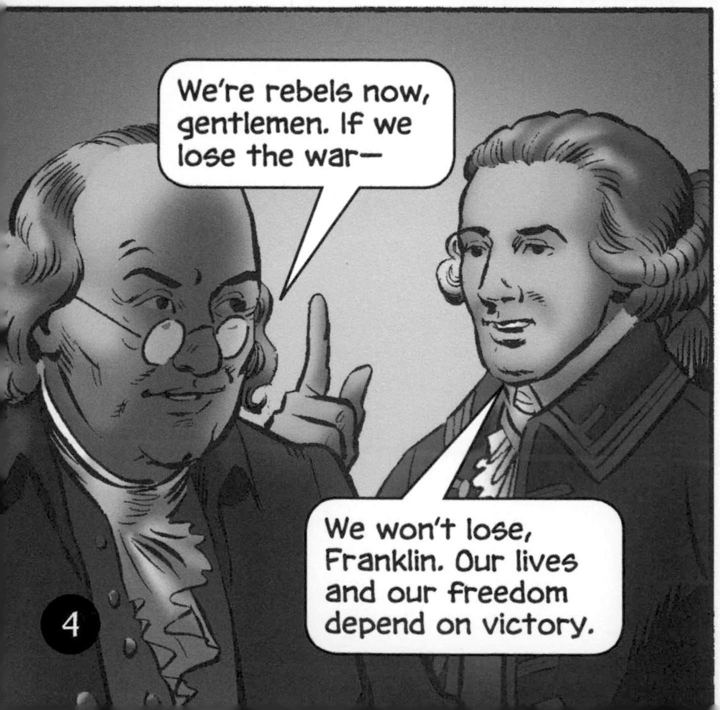
We're rebels now, gentlemen. If we lose the war—
We won't lose, Franklin. Our lives and our freedom depend on victory.

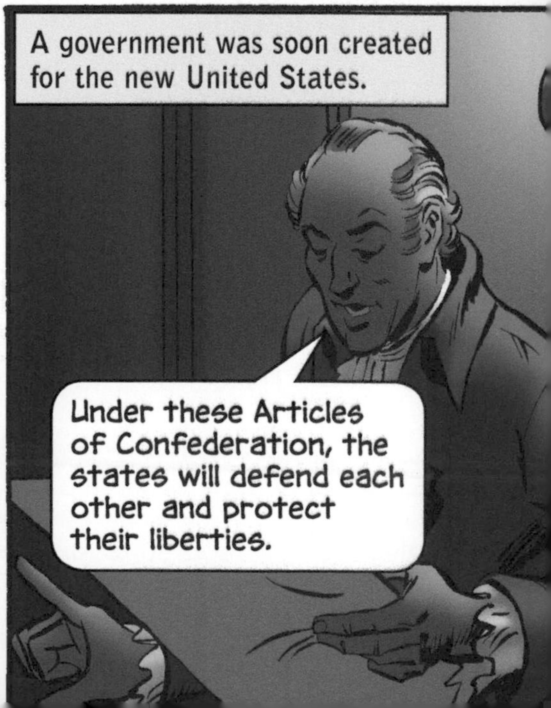
A government was soon created for the new United States.
Under these Articles of Confederation, the states will defend each other and protect their liberties.

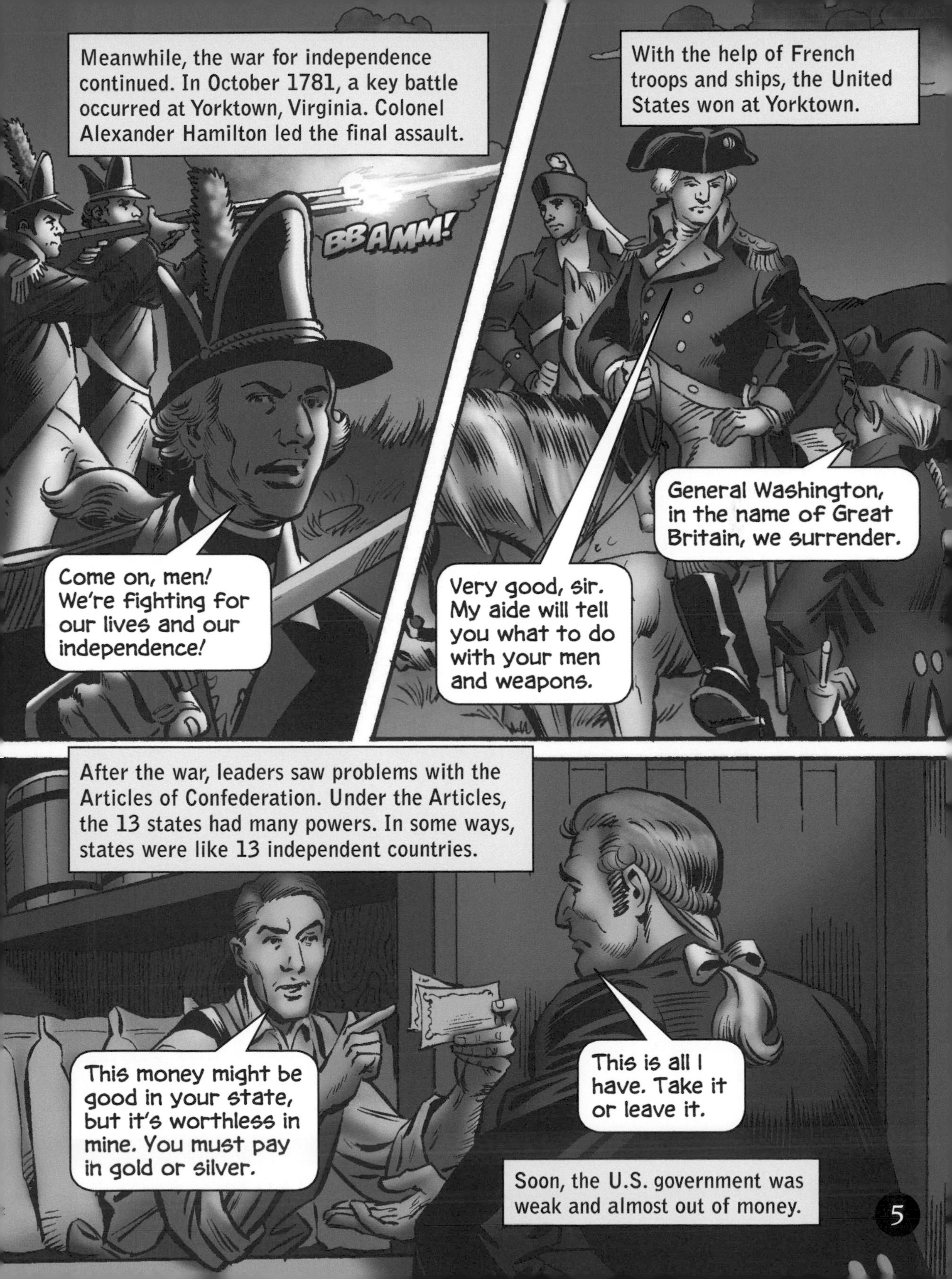
Meanwhile, the war for independence continued. In October 1781, a key battle occurred at Yorktown, Virginia. Colonel Alexander Hamilton led the final assault.
BBAMM!
Come on, men! We're fighting for our lives and our independence!
With the help of French troops and ships, the United States won at Yorktown.
General Washington, in the name of Great Britain, we surrender.
Very good, sir. My aide will tell you what to do with your men and weapons.
After the war, leaders saw problems with the Articles of Confederation. Under the Articles, the 13 states had many powers. In some ways, states were like 13 independent countries.
This money might be good in your state, but it's worthless in mine. You must pay in gold or silver.
This is all I have. Take it or leave it.
Soon, the U.S. government was weak and almost out of money.

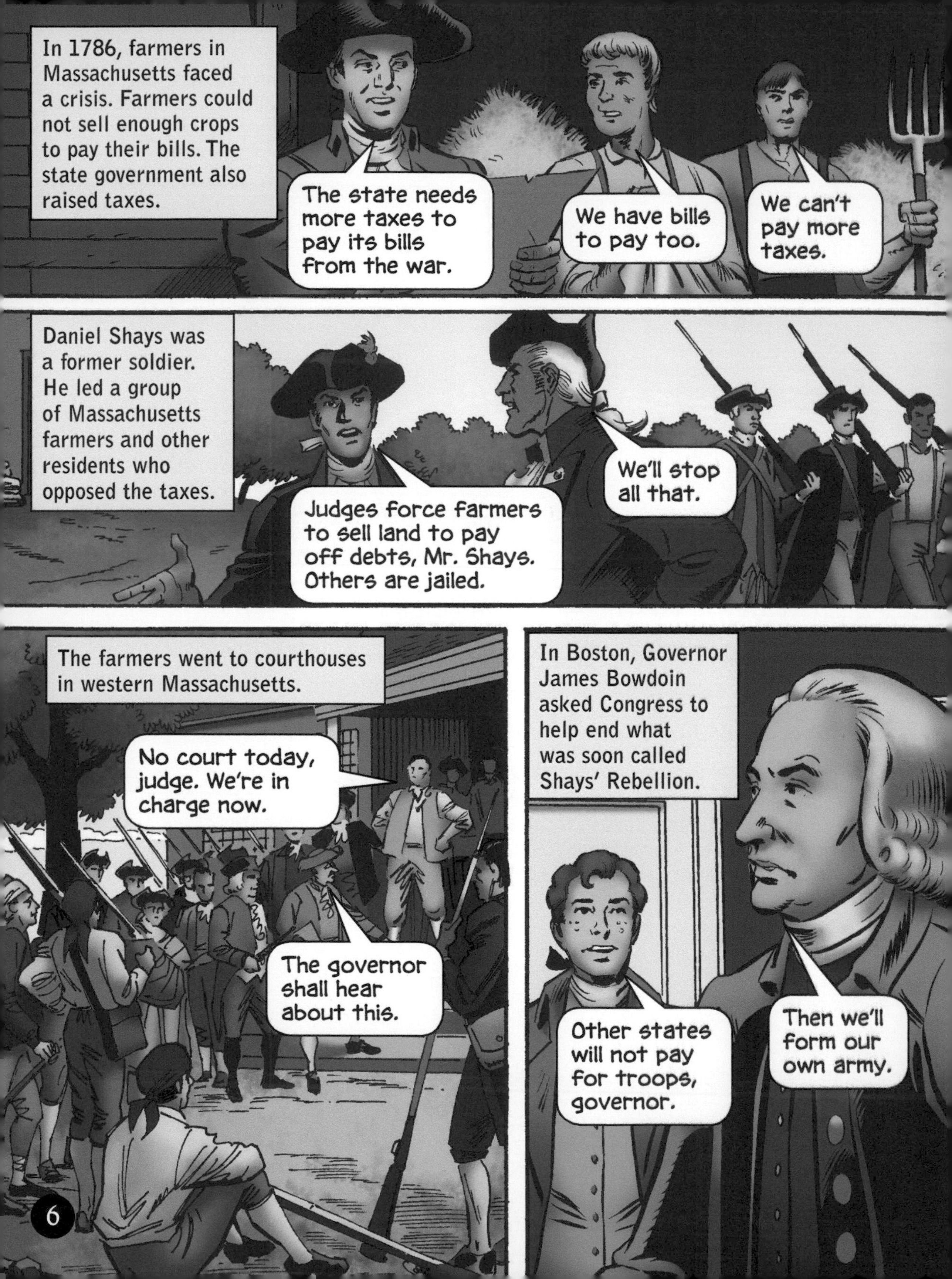

In 1786, farmers in Massachusetts faced a crisis. Farmers could not sell enough crops to pay their bills. The state government also raised taxes.
The state needs more taxes to pay its bills from the war.
We have bills to pay too.
We can't pay more taxes.
Daniel Shays was a former soldier. He led a group of Massachusetts farmers and other residents who opposed the taxes.
Judges force farmers to sell land to pay off debts, Mr. Shays. Others are jailed.
We'll stop all that.
The farmers went to courthouses in western Massachusetts.
No court today, judge. We're in charge now.
The governor shall hear about this.
In Boston, Governor James Bowdoin asked Congress to help end what was soon called Shays' Rebellion.
Other states will not pay for troops, governor.
Then we'll form our own army.

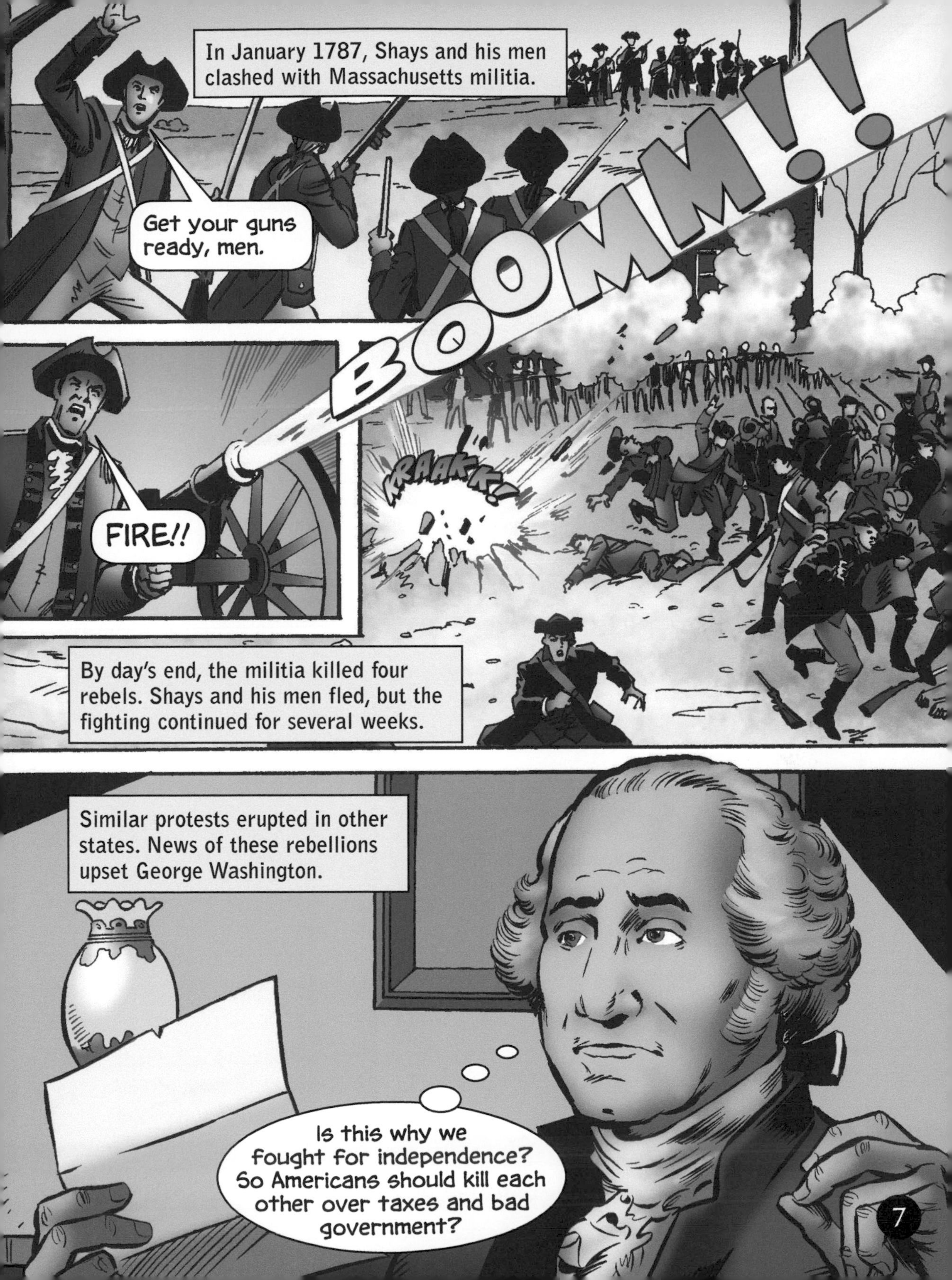

In January 1787, Shays and his men clashed with Massachusetts militia.
Get your guns ready, men.
BOOMM!!!
FIRE!!
KRAAKK!
By day's end, the militia killed four rebels. Shays and his men fled, but the fighting continued for several weeks.
Similar protests erupted in other states. News of these rebellions upset George Washington.
Is this why we fought for independence? So Americans should kill each other over taxes and bad government?

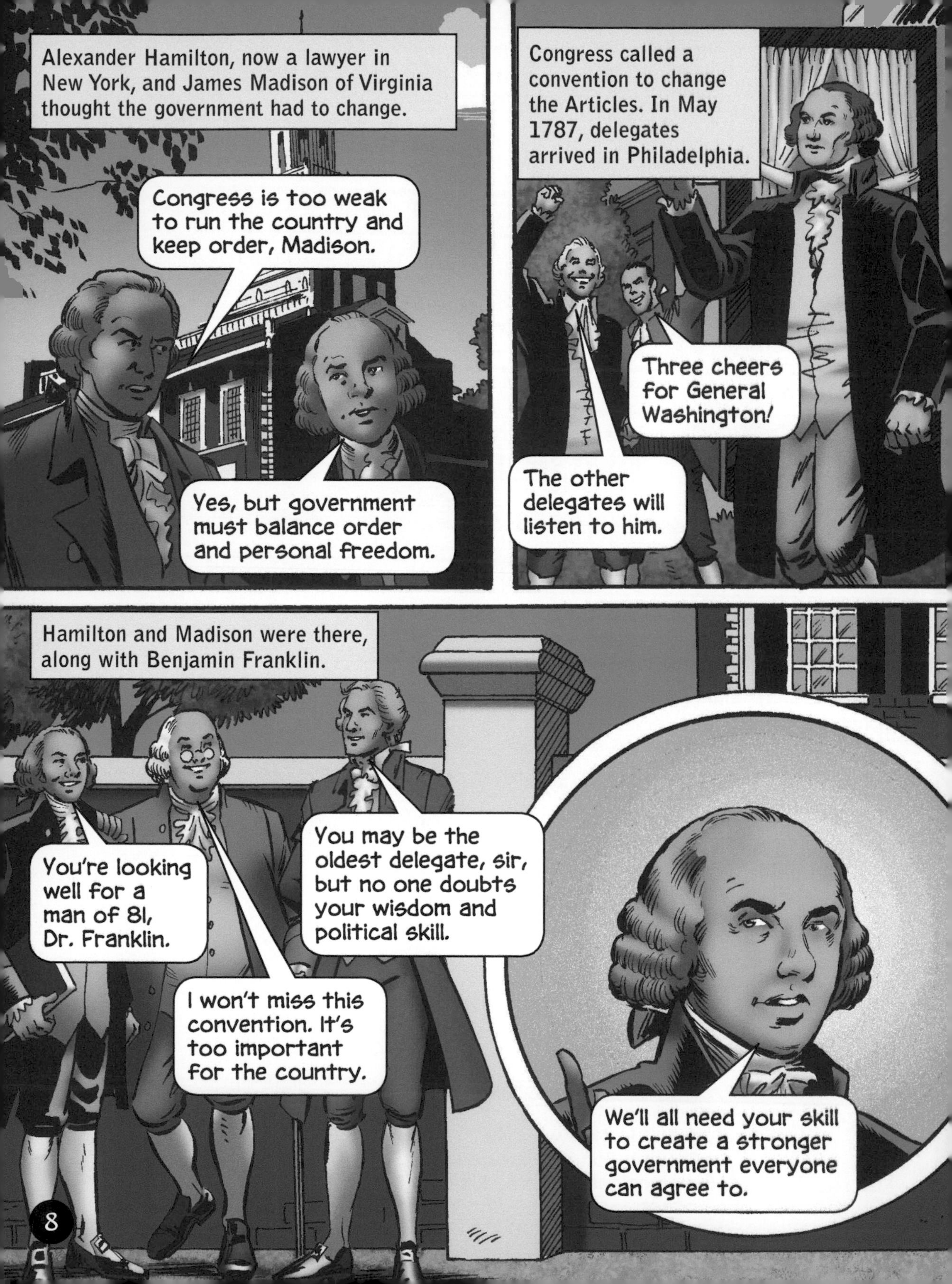

Alexander Hamilton, now a lawyer in New York, and James Madison of Virginia thought the government had to change.
Congress is too weak to run the country and keep order, Madison.
Yes, but government must balance order and personal freedom.
Congress called a convention to change the Articles. In May 1787, delegates arrived in Philadelphia.
Three cheers for General Washington!
The other delegates will listen to him.
Hamilton and Madison were there, along with Benjamin Franklin.
You're looking well for a man of 81, Dr. Franklin.
You may be the oldest delegate, sir, but no one doubts your wisdom and political skill.
I won't miss this convention. It's too important for the country.
We'll all need your skill to create a stronger government everyone can agree to.

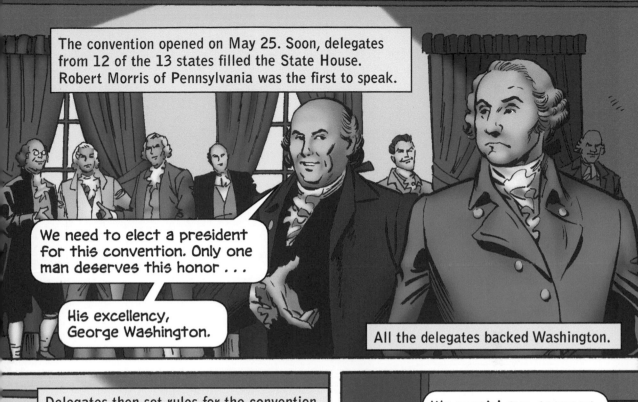

The convention opened on May 25. Soon, delegates from 12 of the 13 states filled the State House. Robert Morris of Pennsylvania was the first to speak.

We need to elect a president for this convention. Only one man deserves this honor . . .

His excellency, George Washington.

All the delegates backed Washington.

Delegates then set rules for the convention.

Delegates may not pass notes to one another. They must not discuss the convention outside the State House.

Sir, are all these rules necessary?

We must have secrecy, gentlemen. Otherwise, the citizens might try to influence what we say and do.

If we are to succeed, then everyone must say what he really believes.

With the secrecy agreement in place, the delegates freely debated each other over the long, hot summer.

CHAPTER 2

CREATING THE CONSTITUTION

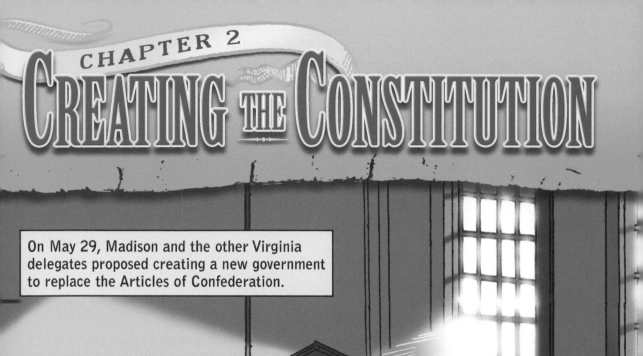

On May 29, Madison and the other Virginia delegates proposed creating a new government to replace the Articles of Confederation.

The Articles are not working. We must have one government that unites us all.

We are proposing a new government with three branches.

Our Virginia Plan will create a strong national government. One body won't control the government, as Congress does now.

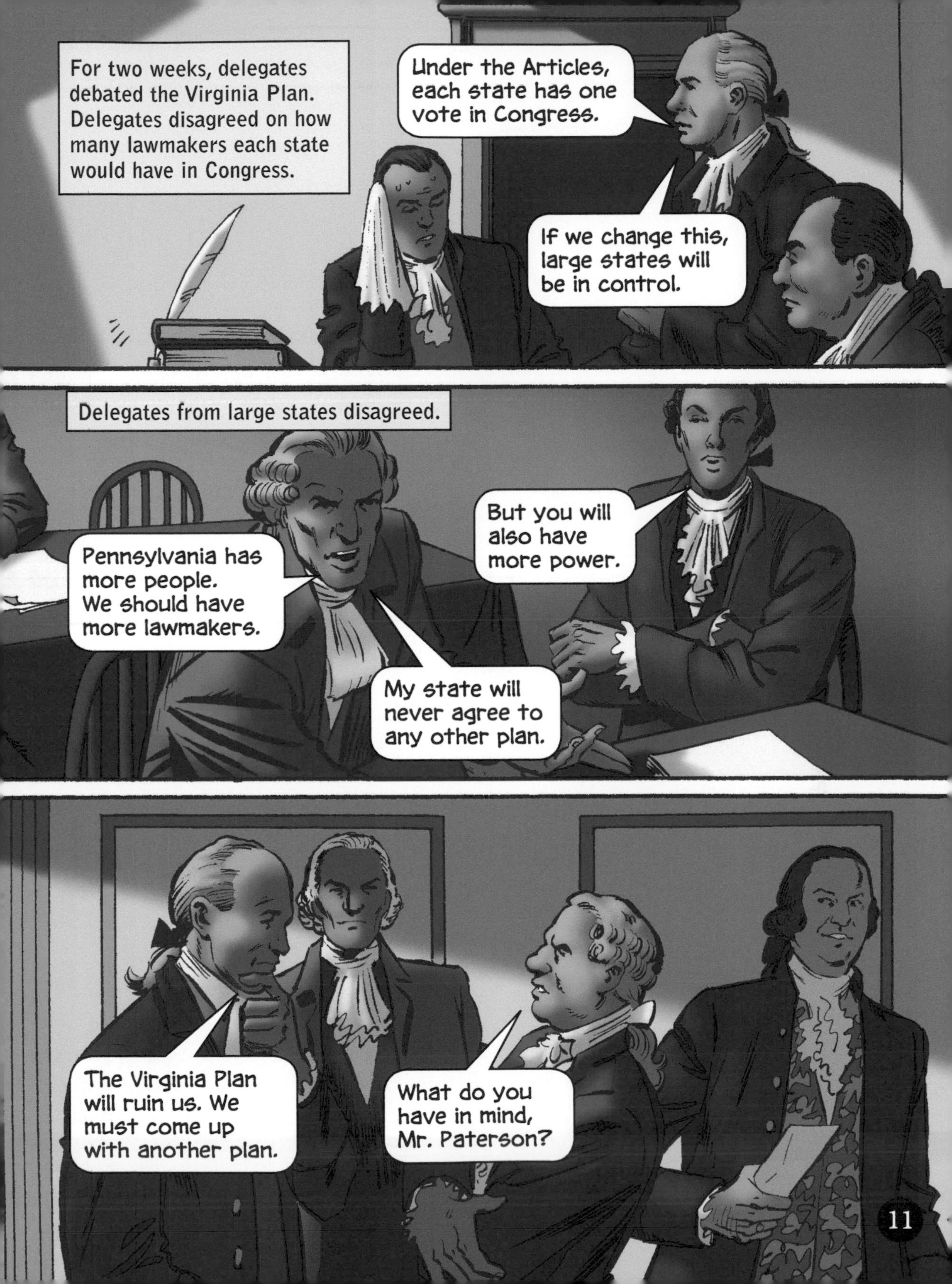
For two weeks, delegates debated the Virginia Plan. Delegates disagreed on how many lawmakers each state would have in Congress.
Under the Articles, each state has one vote in Congress.
If we change this, large states will be in control.
Delegates from large states disagreed.
Pennsylvania has more people. We should have more lawmakers.
But you will also have more power.
My state will never agree to any other plan.
The Virginia Plan will ruin us. We must come up with another plan.
What do you have in mind, Mr. Paterson?

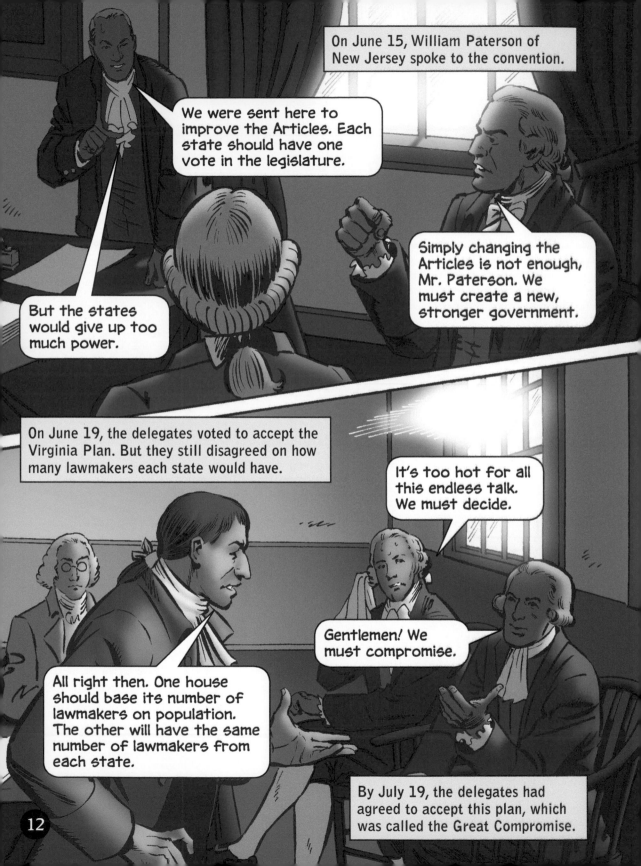

On June 15, William Paterson of New Jersey spoke to the convention.

We were sent here to improve the Articles. Each state should have one vote in the legislature.

Simply changing the Articles is not enough, Mr. Paterson. We must create a new, stronger government.

But the states would give up too much power.

On June 19, the delegates voted to accept the Virginia Plan. But they still disagreed on how many lawmakers each state would have.

It's too hot for all this endless talk. We must decide.

Gentlemen! We must compromise.

All right then. One house should base its number of lawmakers on population. The other will have the same number of lawmakers from each state.

By July 19, the delegates had agreed to accept this plan, which was called the Great Compromise.

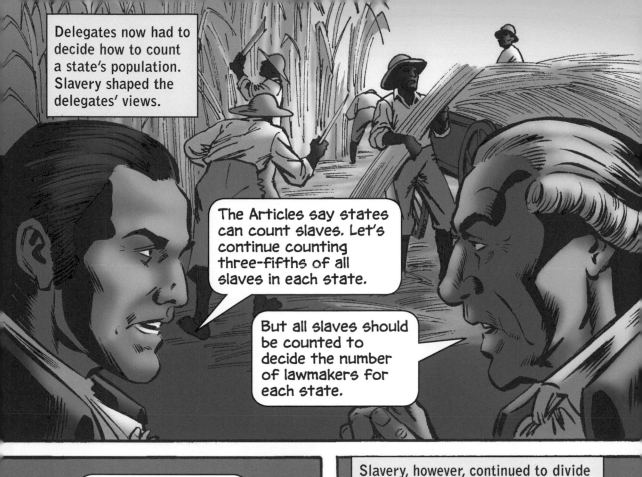

Delegates now had to decide how to count a state's population. Slavery shaped the delegates' views.

The Articles say states can count slaves. Let's continue counting three-fifths of all slaves in each state.

But all slaves should be counted to decide the number of lawmakers for each state.

So, will you count slaves the same way for your taxes?

Of course not!

Delegates decided to count three-fifths of a state's slaves for population and taxes.

Slavery, however, continued to divide the delegates. Some Northerners wanted to end the slave trade, which brought new slaves into the country.

Gentlemen, we can't risk breaking apart the convention over slavery.

The delegates finally agreed to continue the international slave trade for 20 more years.

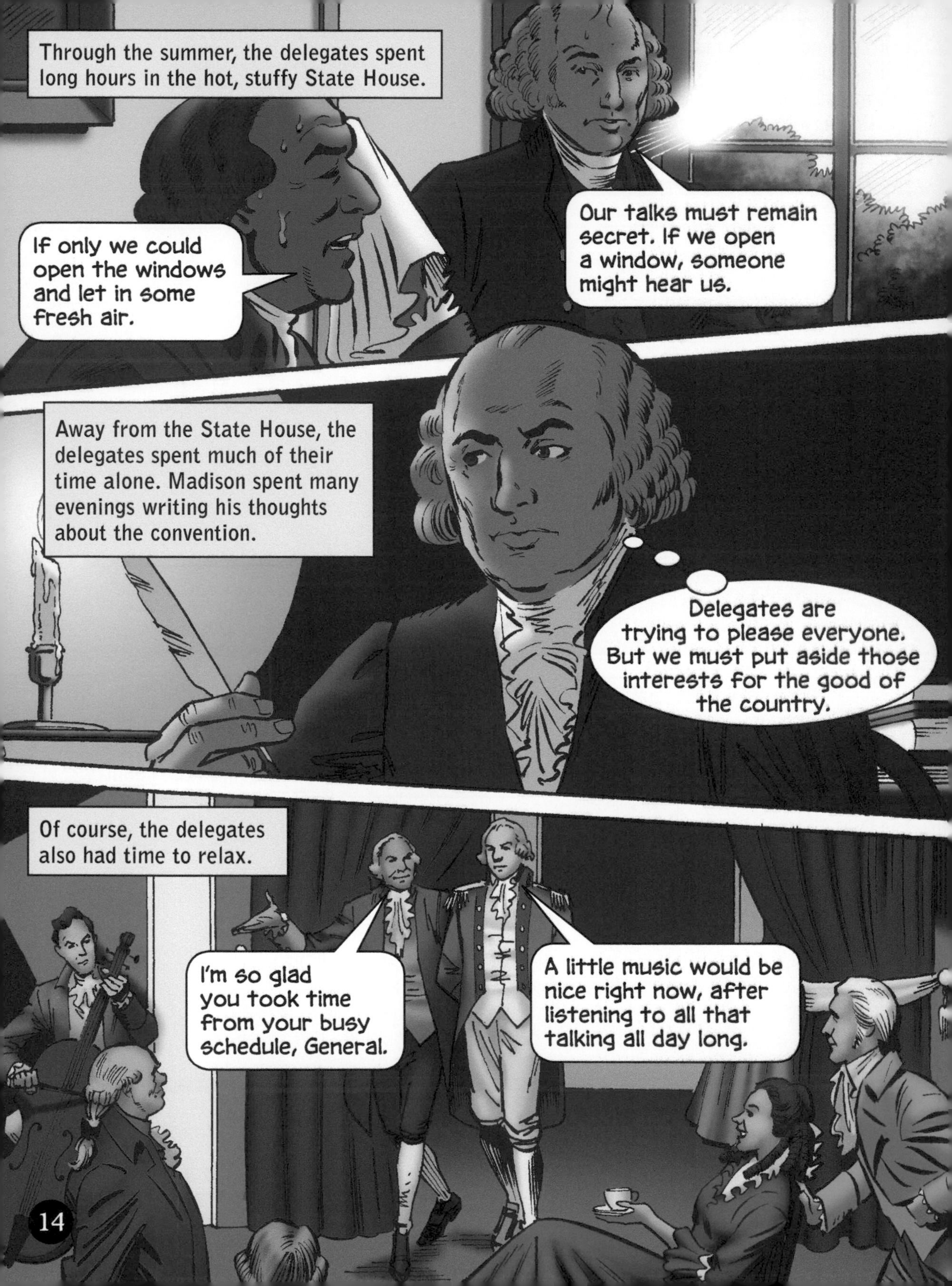
Through the summer, the delegates spent long hours in the hot, stuffy State House.
If only we could open the windows and let in some fresh air.
Our talks must remain secret. If we open a window, someone might hear us.
Away from the State House, the delegates spent much of their time alone. Madison spent many evenings writing his thoughts about the convention.
Delegates are trying to please everyone. But we must put aside those interests for the good of the country.
Of course, the delegates also had time to relax.
I'm so glad you took time from your busy schedule, General.
A little music would be nice right now, after listening to all that talking all day long.

At the end of July, a group of delegates looked over all the issues discussed during the convention. The group then wrote a Constitution for a new government.

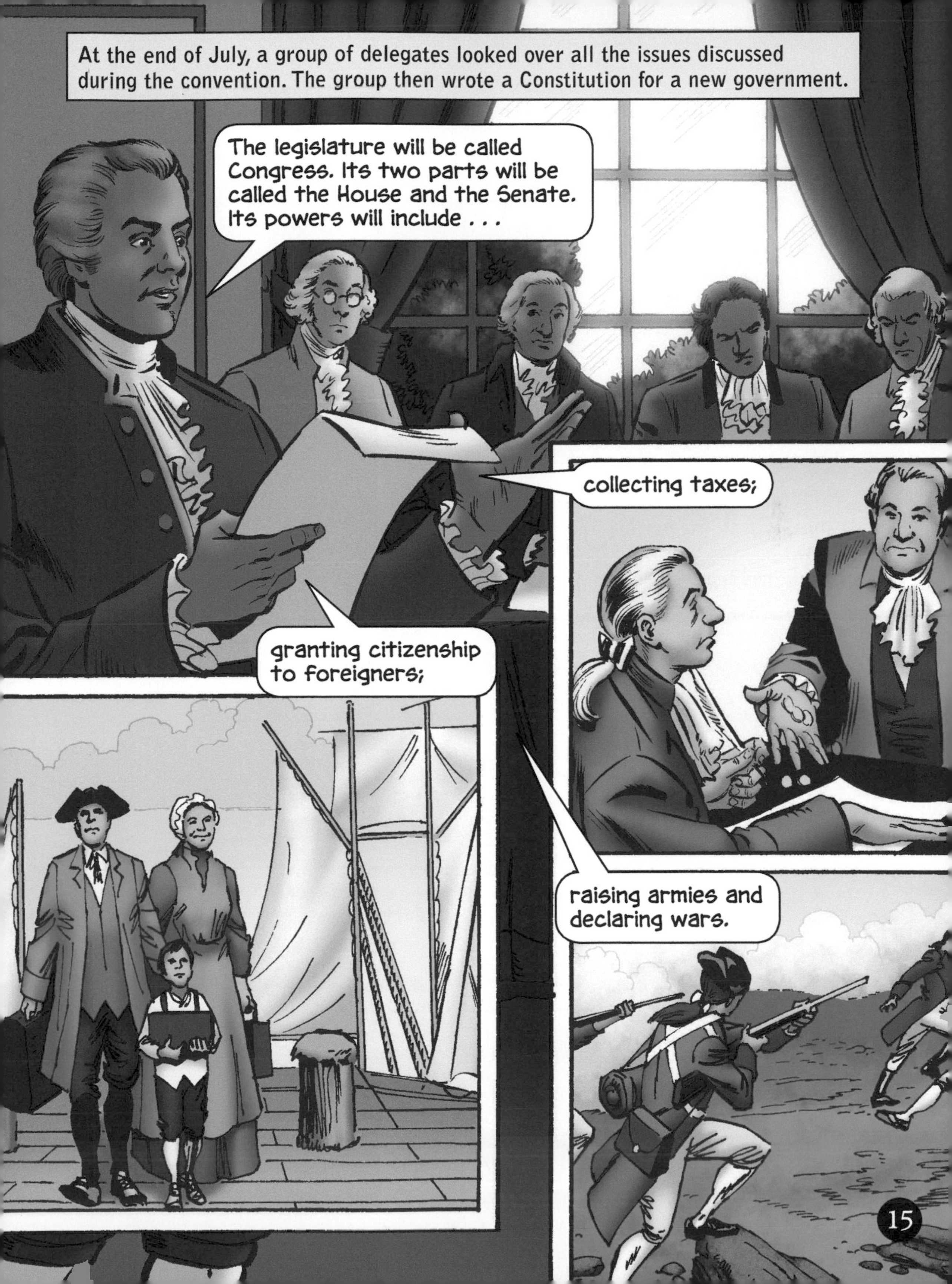
The legislature will be called Congress. Its two parts will be called the House and the Senate. Its powers will include . . .
collecting taxes;
granting citizenship to foreigners;
raising armies and declaring wars.

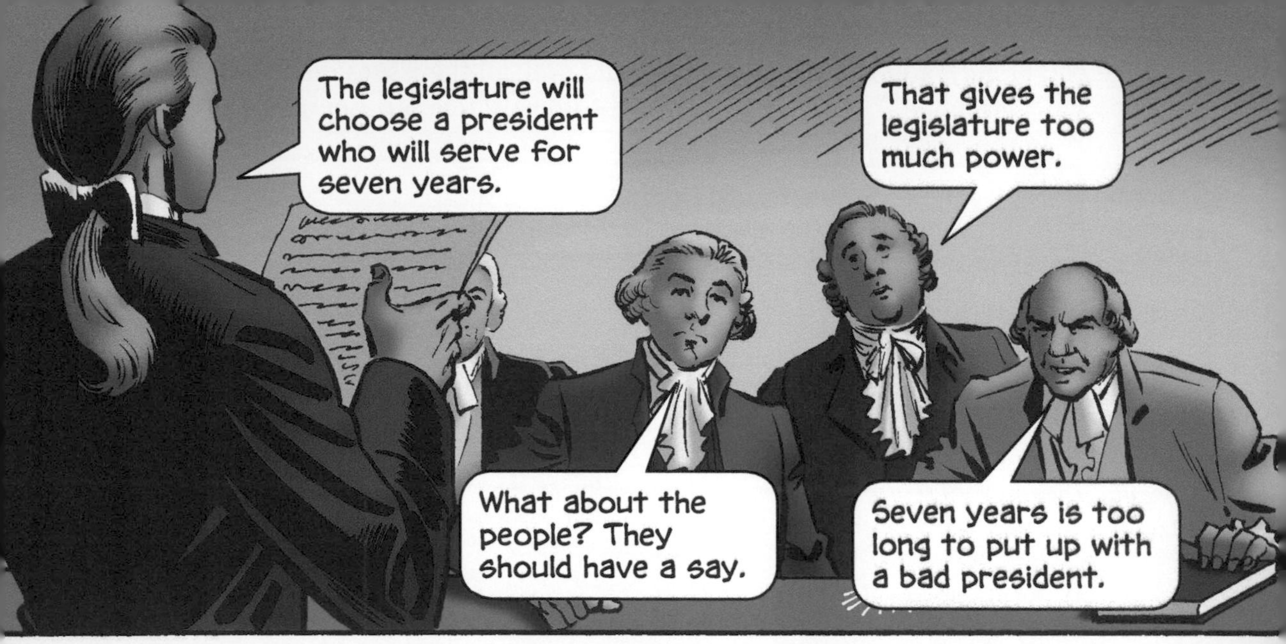
The legislature will choose a president who will serve for seven years.
That gives the legislature too much power.
What about the people? They should have a say.
Seven years is too long to put up with a bad president.

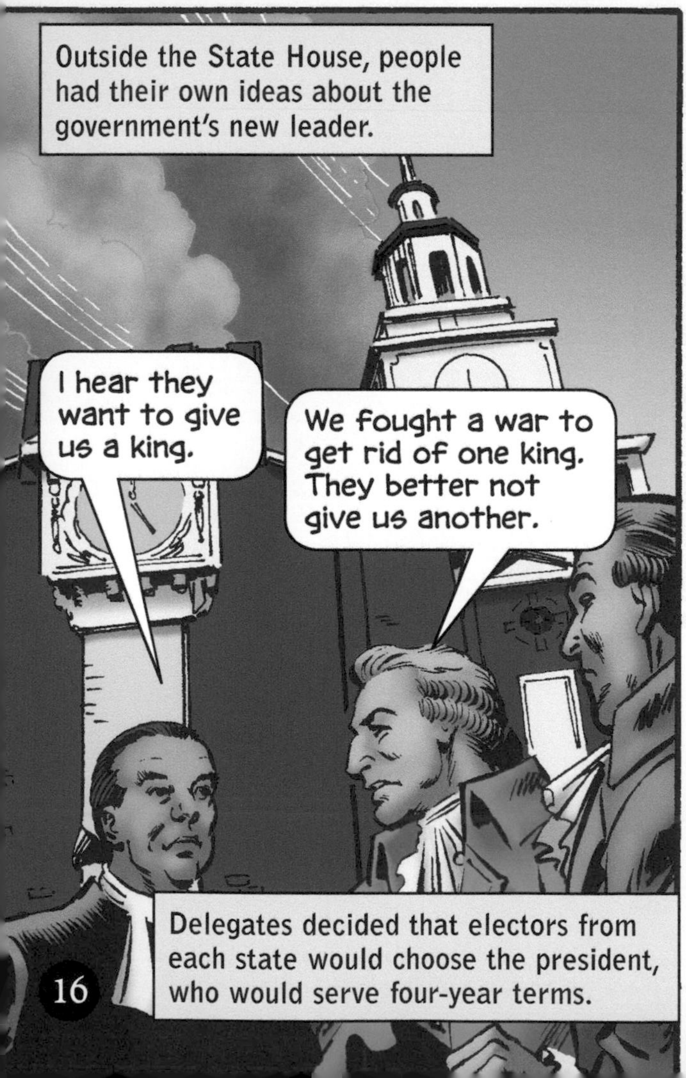
Outside the State House, people had their own ideas about the government's new leader.
I hear they want to give us a king.
We fought a war to get rid of one king. They better not give us another.
Delegates decided that electors from each state would choose the president, who would serve four-year terms.

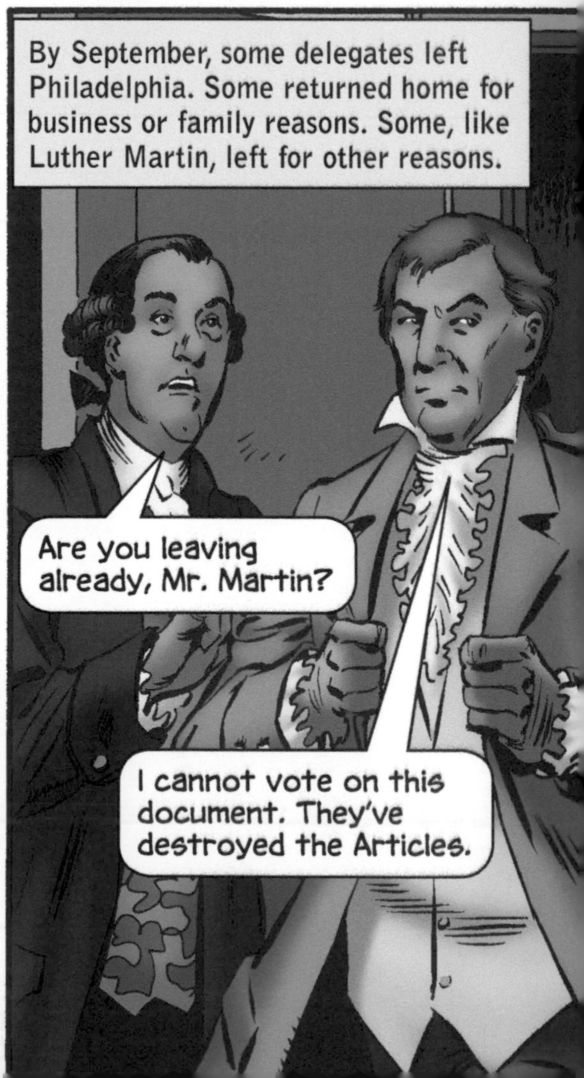
By September, some delegates left Philadelphia. Some returned home for business or family reasons. Some, like Luther Martin, left for other reasons.
Are you leaving already, Mr. Martin?
I cannot vote on this document. They've destroyed the Articles.

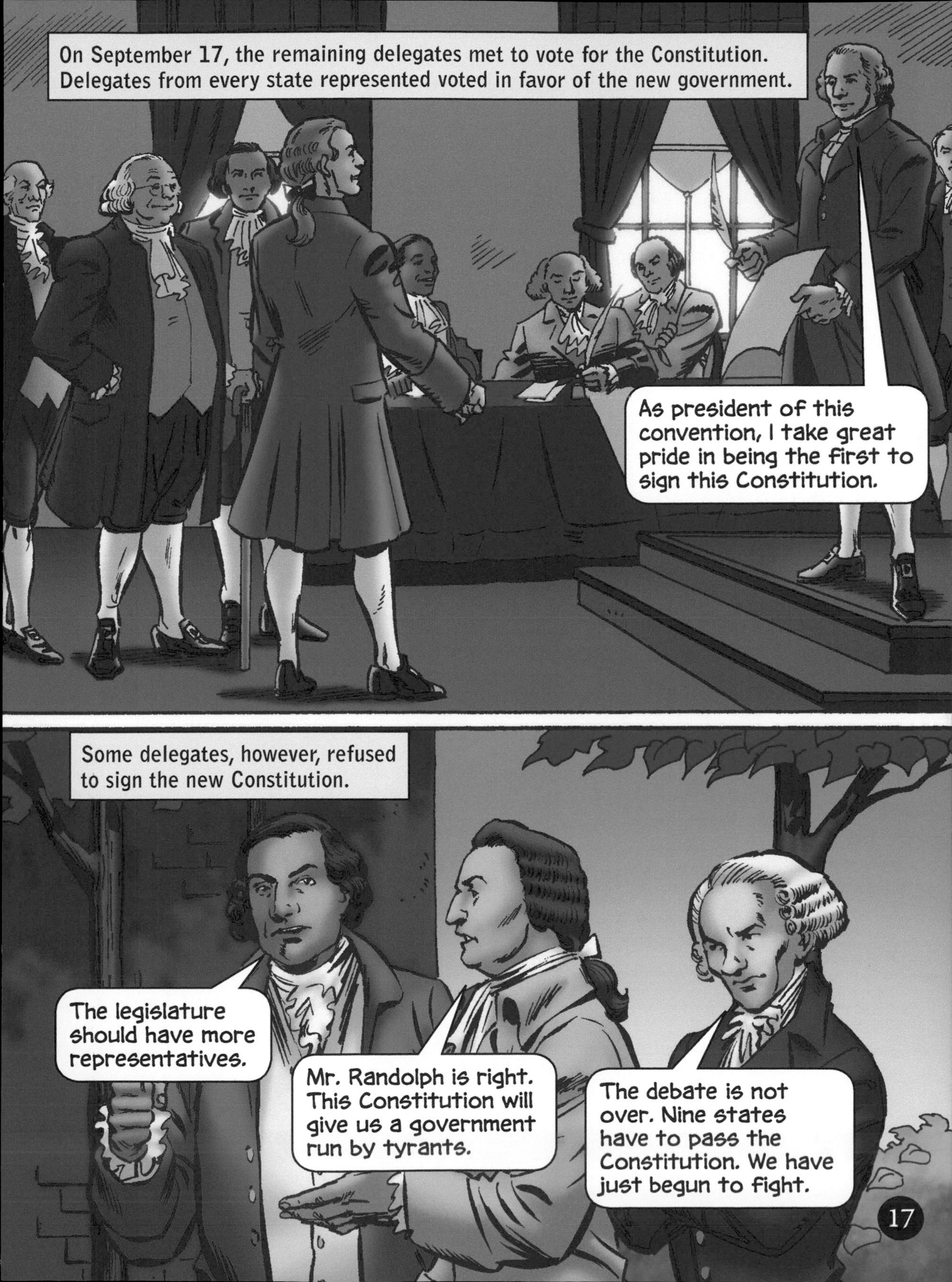
On September 17, the remaining delegates met to vote for the Constitution. Delegates from every state represented voted in favor of the new government.
As president of this convention, I take great pride in being the first to sign this Constitution.
Some delegates, however, refused to sign the new Constitution.
The legislature should have more representatives.
Mr. Randolph is right. This Constitution will give us a government run by tyrants.
The debate is not over. Nine states have to pass the Constitution. We have just begun to fight.

CHAPTER 3

BATTLE IN THE STATES

The debate over the Constitution began quickly. Supporters of the Constitution called themselves Federalists. They included George Washington. George Mason and others who opposed the Constitution were called Anti-Federalists.

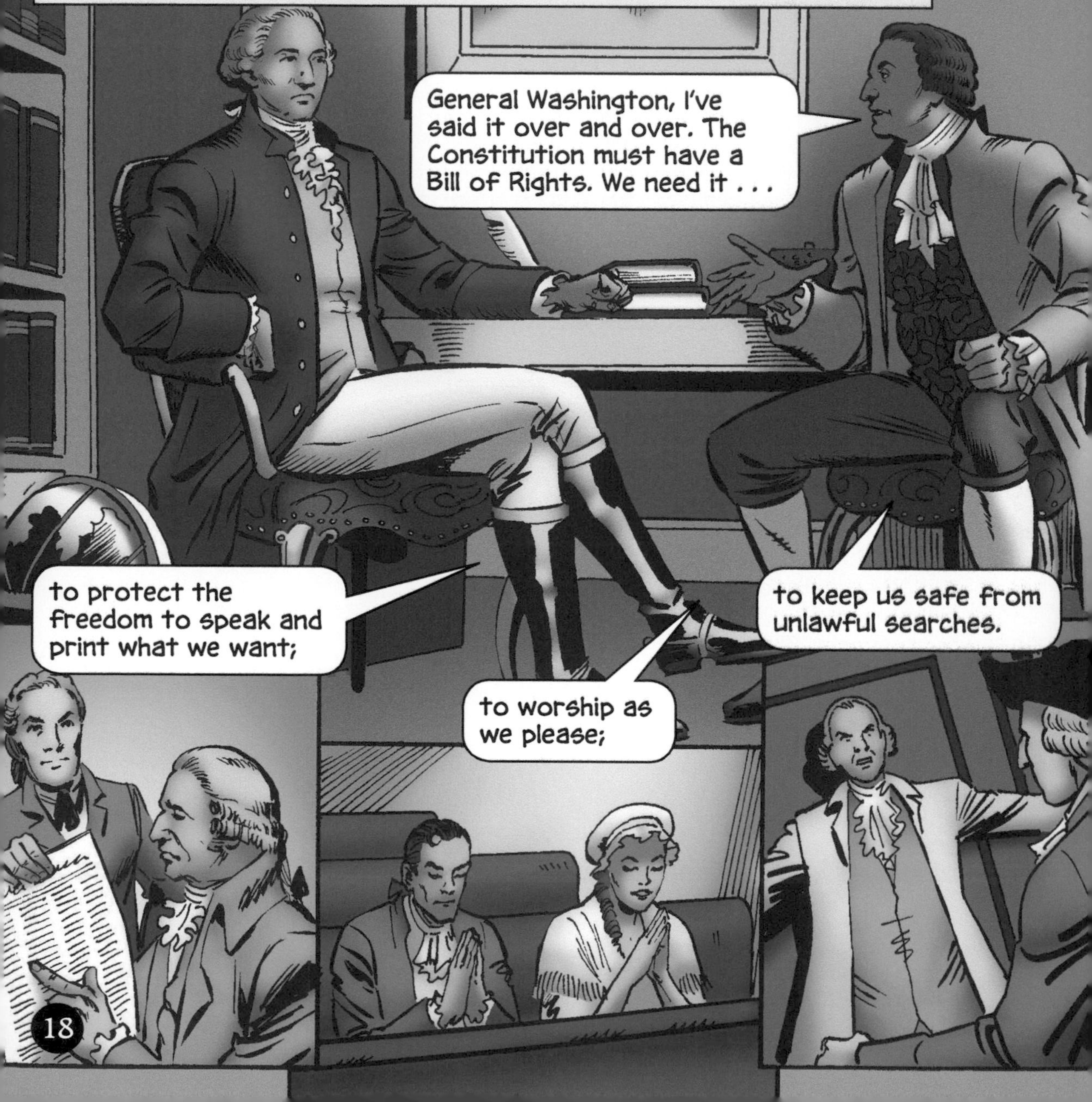
General Washington, I've said it over and over. The Constitution must have a Bill of Rights. We need it . . .
to protect the freedom to speak and print what we want;
to worship as we please;
to keep us safe from unlawful searches.

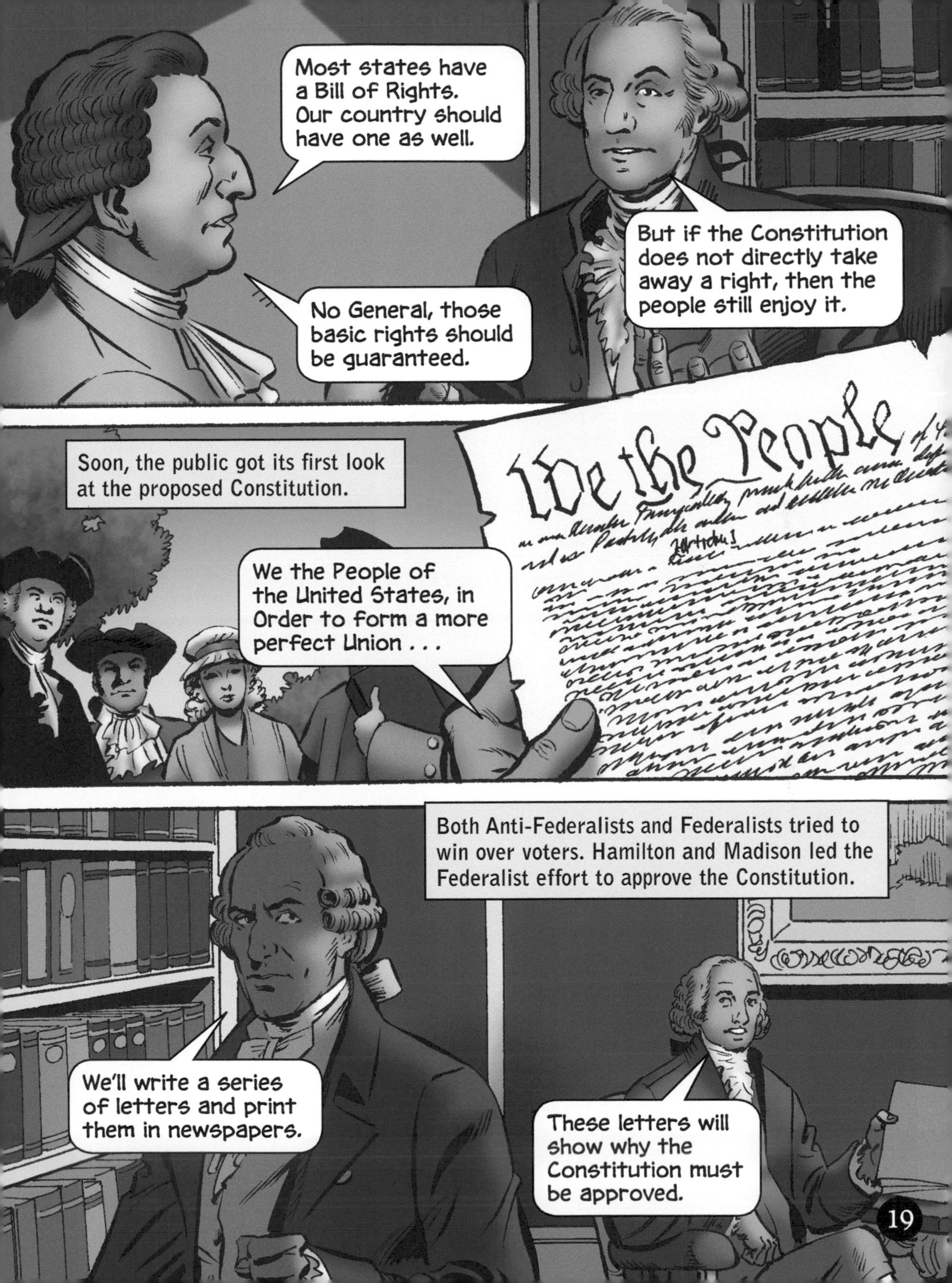

Most states have a Bill of Rights. Our country should have one as well.
But if the Constitution does not directly take away a right, then the people still enjoy it.
No General, those basic rights should be guaranteed.
Soon, the public got its first look at the proposed Constitution.
We the People
We the People of the United States, in Order to form a more perfect Union . . .
Both Anti-Federalists and Federalists tried to win over voters. Hamilton and Madison led the Federalist effort to approve the Constitution.
We'll write a series of letters and print them in newspapers.
These letters will show why the Constitution must be approved.

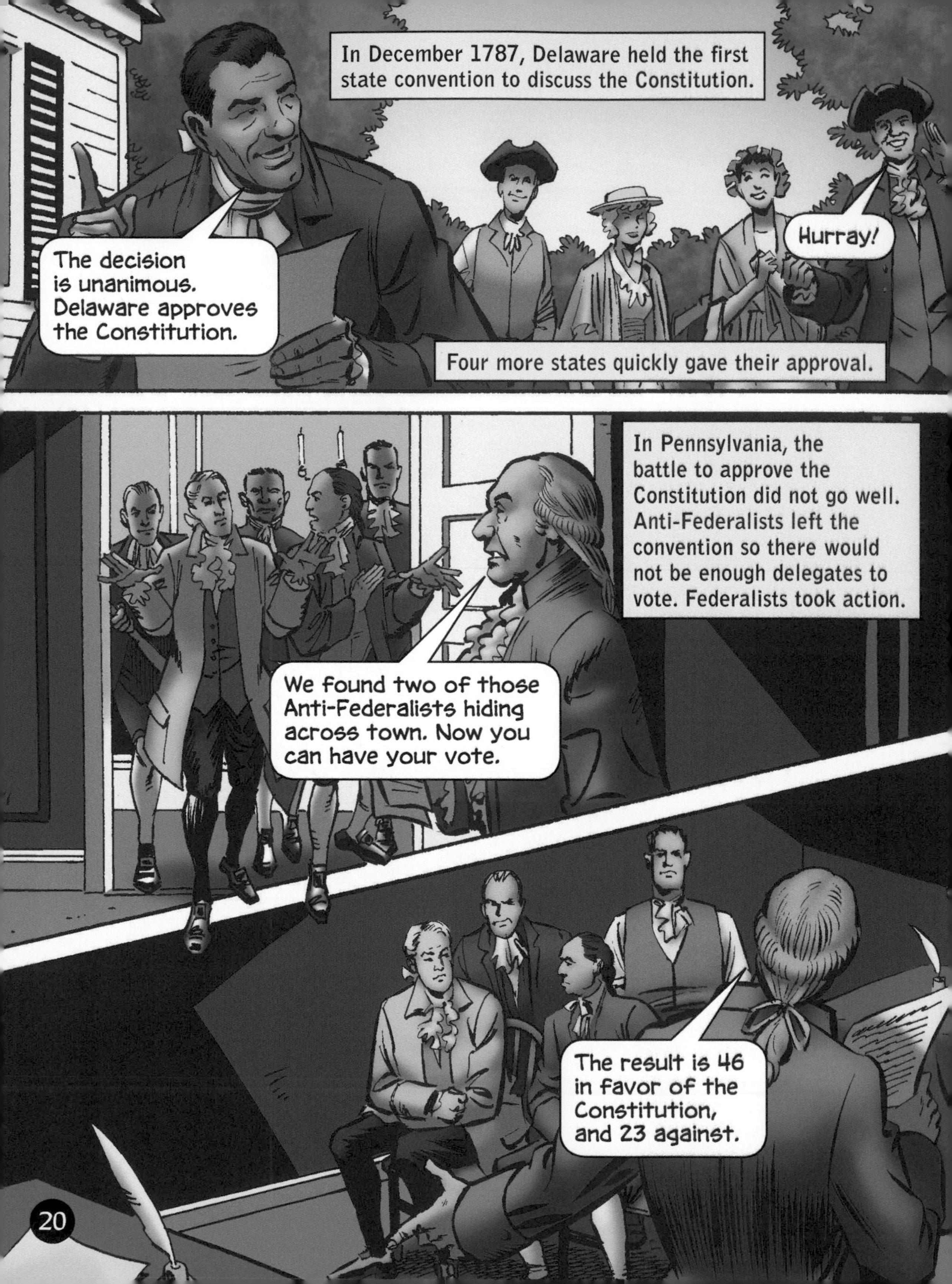

In December 1787, Delaware held the first state convention to discuss the Constitution.
The decision is unanimous. Delaware approves the Constitution.
Hurray!
Four more states quickly gave their approval.
In Pennsylvania, the battle to approve the Constitution did not go well. Anti-Federalists left the convention so there would not be enough delegates to vote. Federalists took action.
We found two of those Anti-Federalists hiding across town. Now you can have your vote.
The result is 46 in favor of the Constitution, and 23 against.

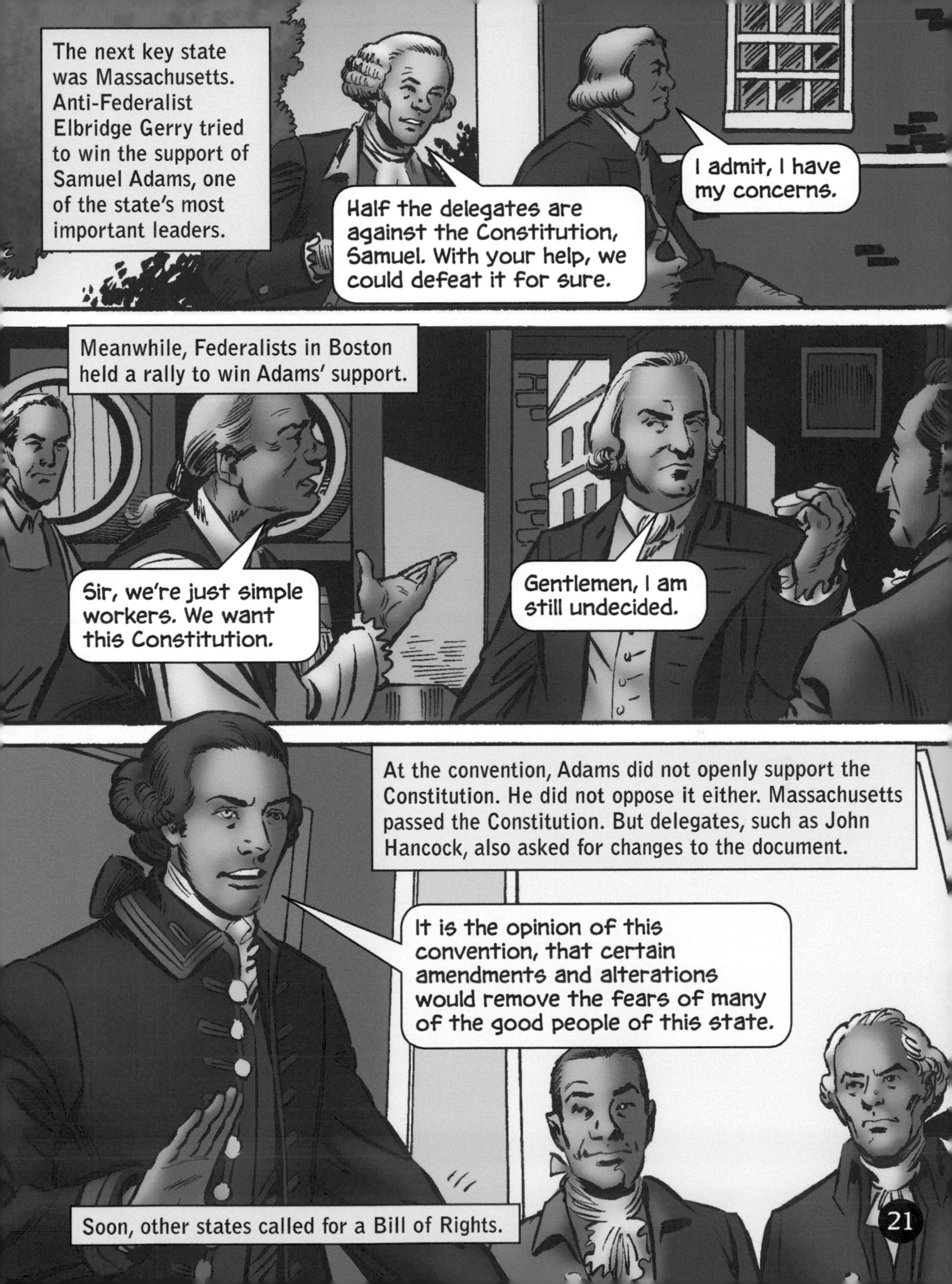

The next key state was Massachusetts. Anti-Federalist Elbridge Gerry tried to win the support of Samuel Adams, one of the state's most important leaders.
Half the delegates are against the Constitution, Samuel. With your help, we could defeat it for sure.
I admit, I have my concerns.
Meanwhile, Federalists in Boston held a rally to win Adams' support.
Sir, we're just simple workers. We want this Constitution.
Gentlemen, I am still undecided.
At the convention, Adams did not openly support the Constitution. He did not oppose it either. Massachusetts passed the Constitution. But delegates, such as John Hancock, also asked for changes to the document.
It is the opinion of this convention, that certain amendments and alterations would remove the fears of many of the good people of this state.
Soon, other states called for a Bill of Rights.

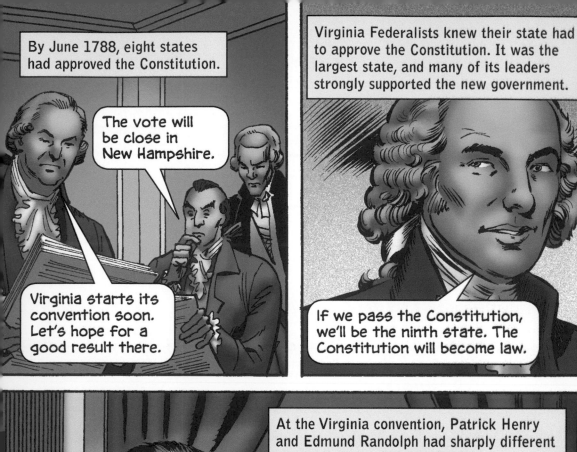

By June 1788, eight states had approved the Constitution.

The vote will be close in New Hampshire.

Virginia starts its convention soon. Let's hope for a good result there.

Virginia Federalists knew their state had to approve the Constitution. It was the largest state, and many of its leaders strongly supported the new government.

If we pass the Constitution, we'll be the ninth state. The Constitution will become law.

At the Virginia convention, Patrick Henry and Edmund Randolph had sharply different views about the Constitution.

The Articles were strong enough to lead us to victory against Great Britain. Who knows the dangers of this new system?

Is this Constitution perfect? Of course not, Mr. Henry. I once opposed it. But I now believe it will give our country a government as strong as Virginia's.

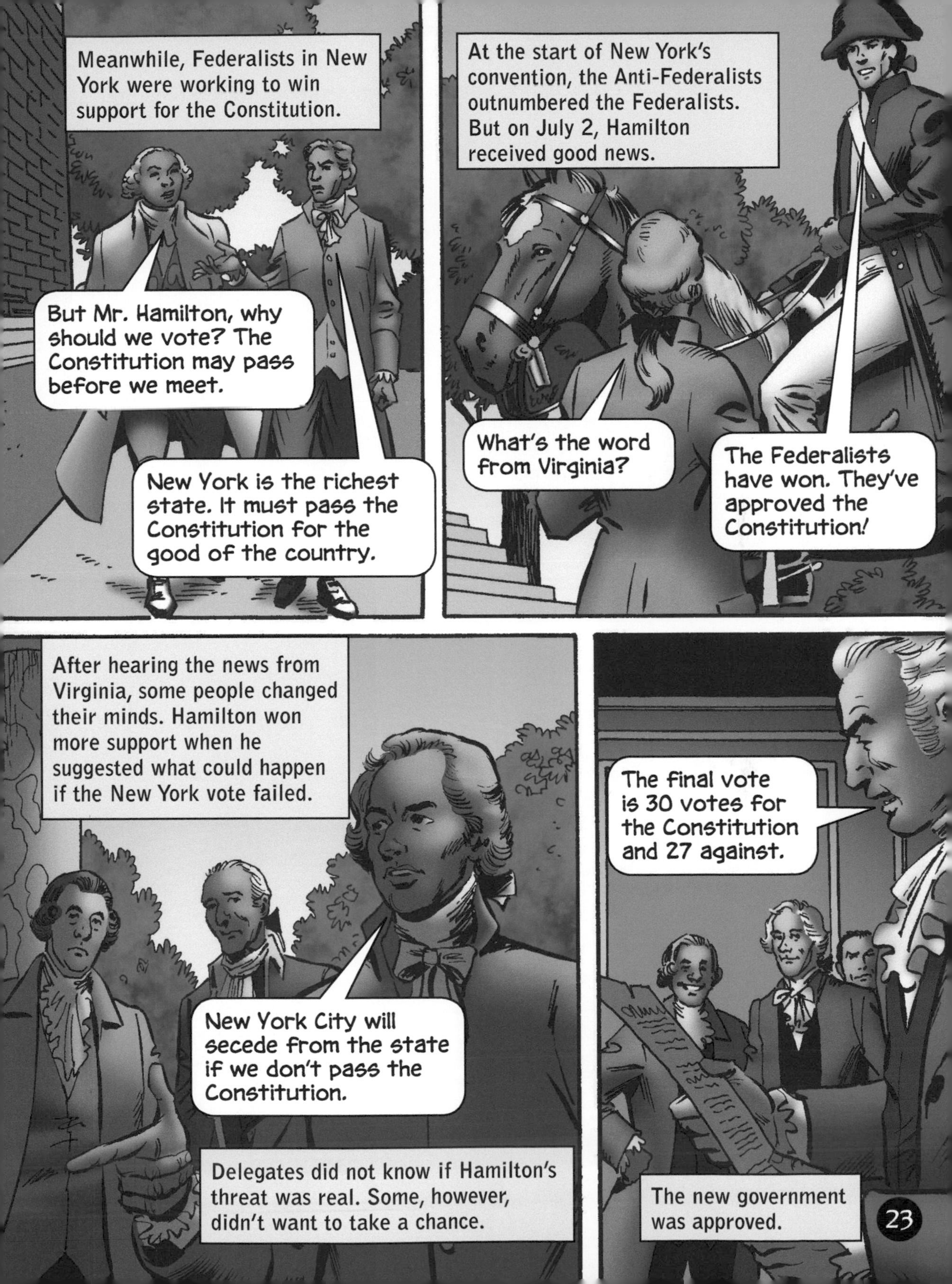
Meanwhile, Federalists in New York were working to win support for the Constitution.
But Mr. Hamilton, why should we vote? The Constitution may pass before we meet.
New York is the richest state. It must pass the Constitution for the good of the country.
At the start of New York's convention, the Anti-Federalists outnumbered the Federalists. But on July 2, Hamilton received good news.
What's the word from Virginia?
The Federalists have won. They've approved the Constitution!
After hearing the news from Virginia, some people changed their minds. Hamilton won more support when he suggested what could happen if the New York vote failed.
New York City will secede from the state if we don't pass the Constitution.
Delegates did not know if Hamilton's threat was real. Some, however, didn't want to take a chance.
The final vote is 30 votes for the Constitution and 27 against.
The new government was approved.

CHAPTER 4

A New Government at Work

During the summer of 1788, Federalists in New York and other cities celebrated the Constitution's approval.

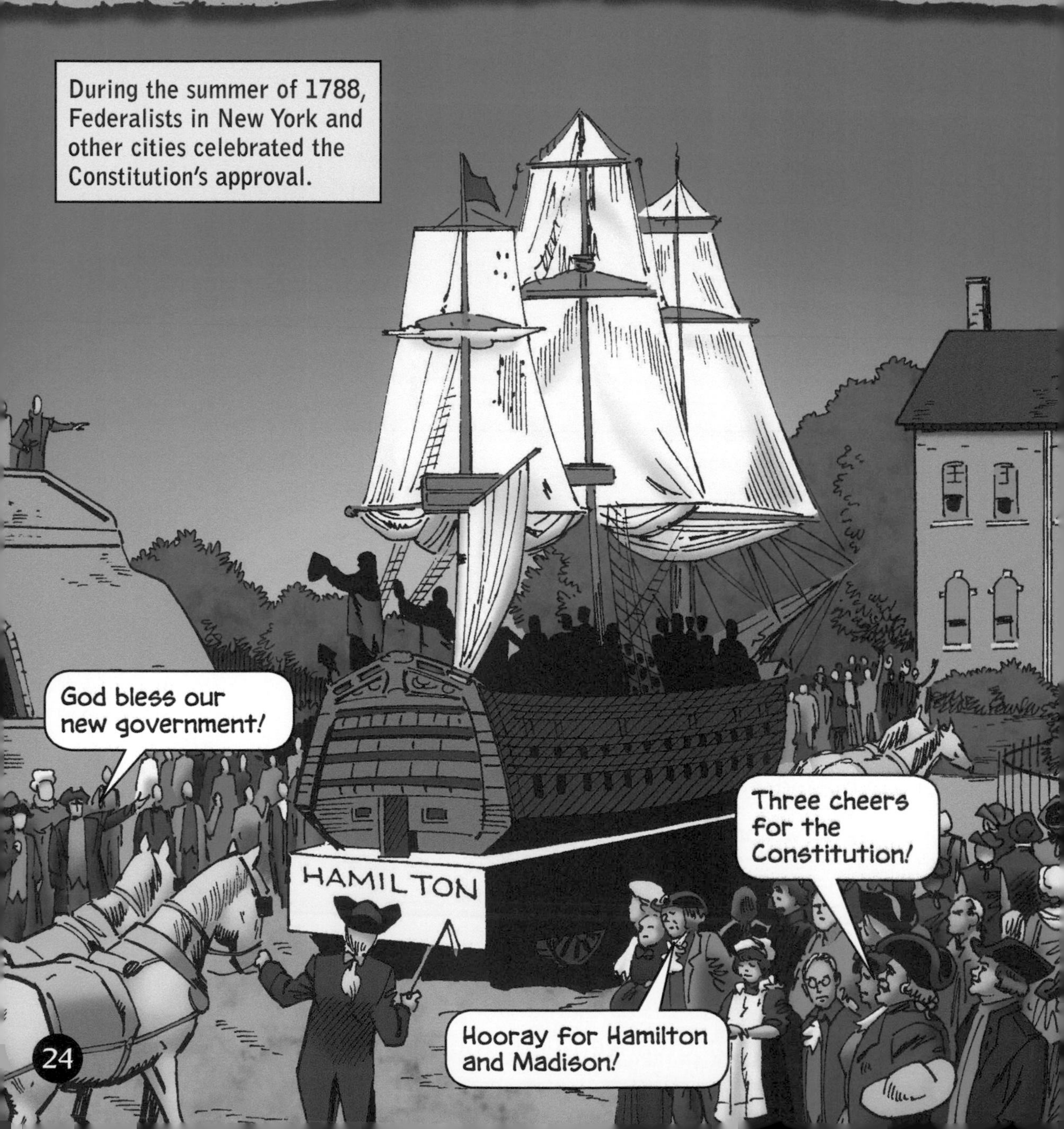

God bless our new government!
HAMILTON
Three cheers for the Constitution!
Hooray for Hamilton and Madison!

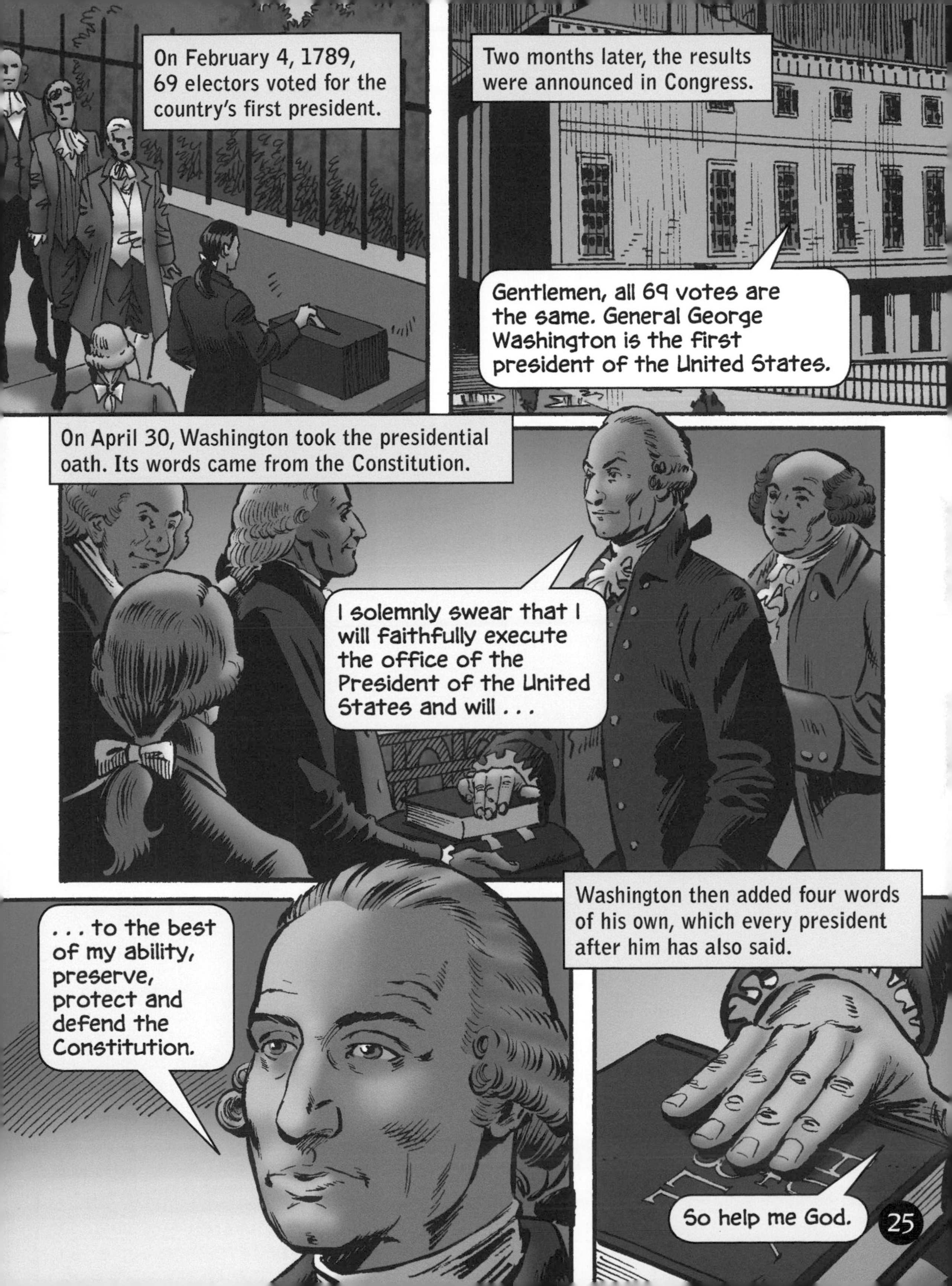
On February 4, 1789, 69 electors voted for the country's first president.
Two months later, the results were announced in Congress.
Gentlemen, all 69 votes are the same. General George Washington is the first president of the United States.
On April 30, Washington took the presidential oath. Its words came from the Constitution.
I solemnly swear that I will faithfully execute the office of the President of the United States and will . . .
. . . to the best of my ability, preserve, protect and defend the Constitution.
Washington then added four words of his own, which every president after him has also said.
So help me God.

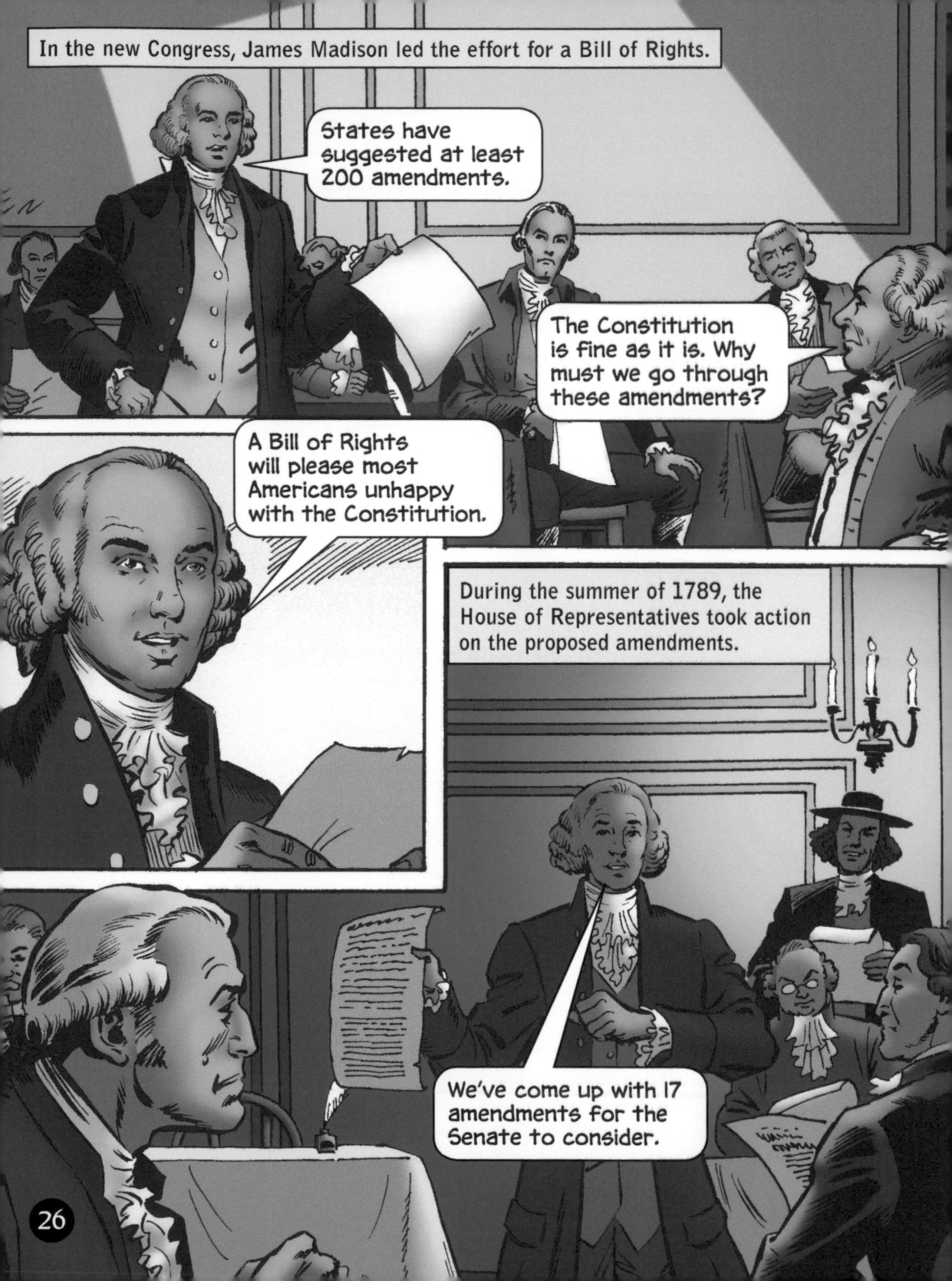

In the new Congress, James Madison led the effort for a Bill of Rights.
States have suggested at least 200 amendments.
The Constitution is fine as it is. Why must we go through these amendments?
A Bill of Rights will please most Americans unhappy with the Constitution.
During the summer of 1789, the House of Representatives took action on the proposed amendments.
We've come up with 17 amendments for the Senate to consider.

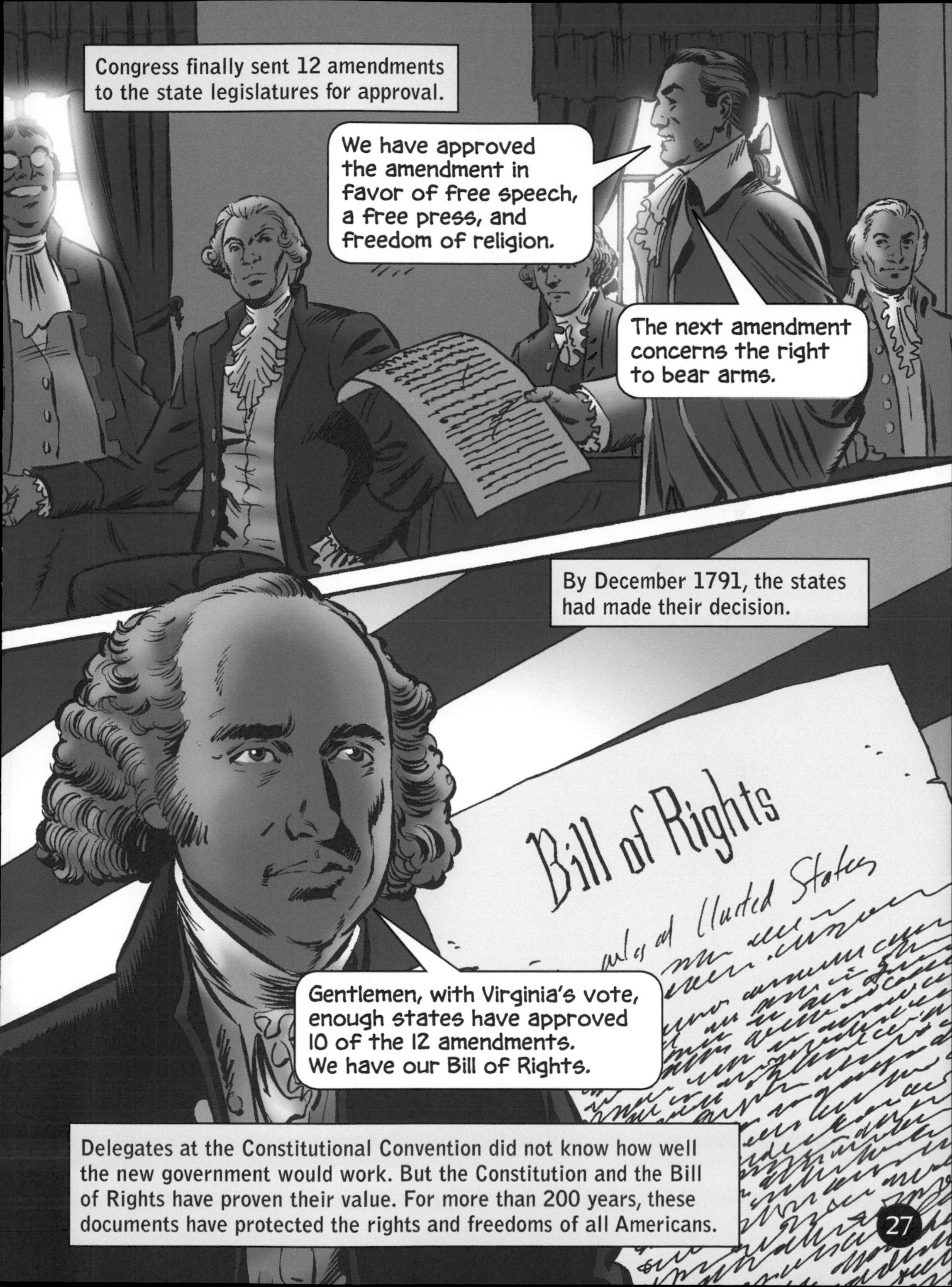
Congress finally sent 12 amendments to the state legislatures for approval.
We have approved the amendment in favor of free speech, a free press, and freedom of religion.
The next amendment concerns the right to bear arms.
By December 1791, the states had made their decision.
Bill of Rights
Gentlemen, with Virginia's vote, enough states have approved 10 of the 12 amendments. We have our Bill of Rights.
Delegates at the Constitutional Convention did not know how well the new government would work. But the Constitution and the Bill of Rights have proven their value. For more than 200 years, these documents have protected the rights and freedoms of all Americans.

More about the U.S. CONSTITUTION

- Thirty-nine names appear on the Constitution, but only 38 men actually signed it. John Dickinson of Delaware left early because he was sick. George Read, also of Delaware, signed the Constitution for him.

- Each state could send as many delegates as it wanted to the Constitutional Convention. Pennsylvania, with eight, had the most. New York had the fewest with three.

- Six men signed both the Declaration of Independence and the Constitution: George Clymer, Benjamin Franklin, Robert Morris, George Read, Roger Sherman, and James Wilson.

- Gouverneur Morris is believed to have written the final version of the Constitution approved at the convention. He worked from a copy written by a committee.

- John Jay, a New York lawyer, joined Alexander Hamilton and James Madison in writing 85 letters in support of the Constitution. Today, these letters are known as the Federalist Papers.

- During Virginia's convention to pass the Constitution, Patrick Henry made several long speeches. He once spoke for seven hours without a break.

- The Bill of Rights passed without the approval of three states. Lawmakers in Connecticut and Georgia were against the Bill of Rights. Massachusetts lawmakers passed most of them, but they never sent official word to Congress. The three states finally approved the Bill of Rights in 1939.
- The original Declaration of Independence, Constitution, and Bill of Rights are on display at the National Archives Building in Washington, D.C. The documents are kept inside special cases that help preserve them.
- Since the Bill of Rights was approved, Congress and the states have passed 17 additional amendments. Some of the most important include the 13th Amendment (1865), which ended slavery, and the 19th Amendment (1920), which gave women the right to vote.

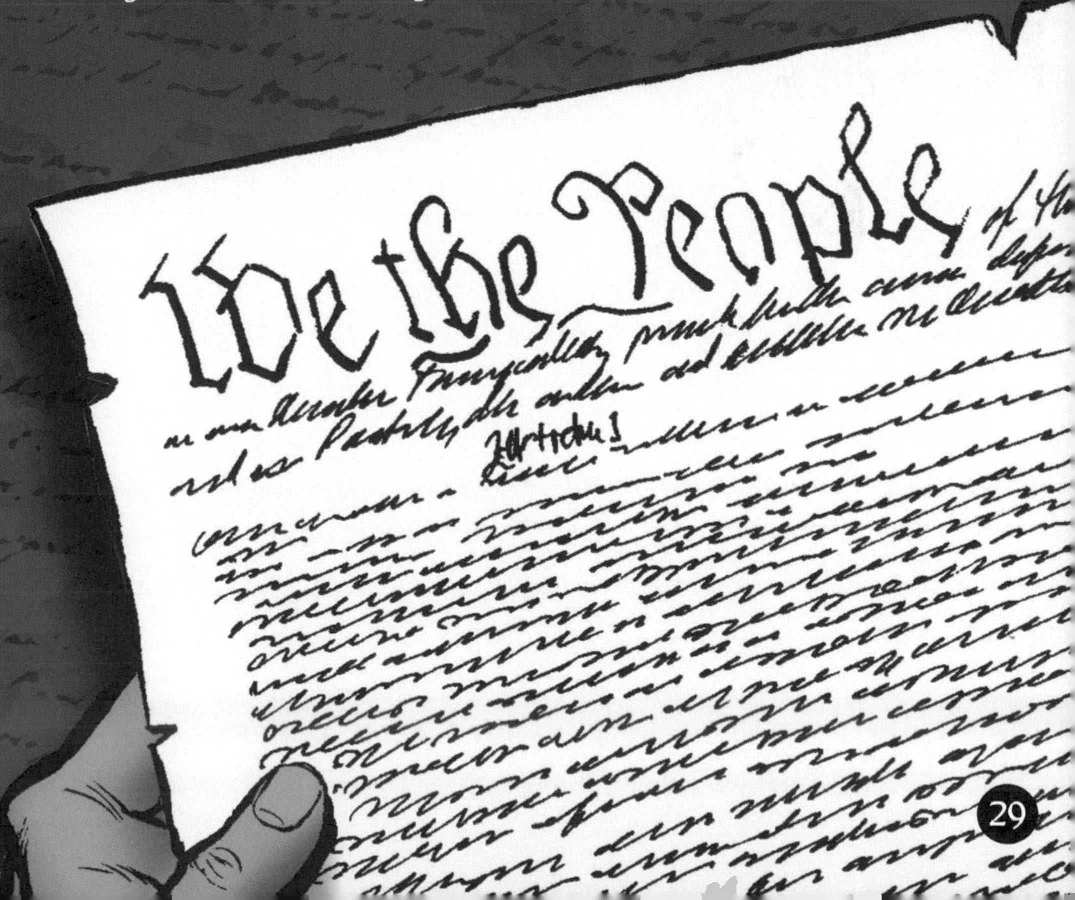

We the People

Glossary

amendment (uh-MEND-muhnt)—a change made to a law or a legal document

constitution (kon-stuh-TOO-shuhn)—the system of laws that state the rights of the people and the powers of the government

delegate (DEL-uh-guht)—person chosen to speak and act for others

oath (OHTH)—a serious, formal promise

right (RITE)—what the law says people can have or do

secede (si-SEED)—to formally withdraw from a group or an organization

Internet Sites

FactHound offers a safe, fun way to find Internet sites related to this book. All of the sites on FactHound have been researched by our staff.

Here's how:
1. Visit *www.facthound.com*
2. Choose your grade level.
3. Type in this book ID **0736864911** for age-appropriate sites. You may also browse subjects by clicking on letters, or by clicking on pictures and words.
4. Click on the **Fetch It** button.

FactHound will fetch the best sites for you!

READ MORE

Doeden, Matt. *George Washington: Leading a New Nation.* Graphic Biographies. Mankato, Minn.: Capstone Press, 2006.

Horn, Geoffrey M. *The Bill of Rights and Other Amendments.* World Almanac Library of American Government. Milwaukee: World Almanac Library, 2004.

Mitchell, Barbara. *Father of the Constitution: A Story about James Madison.* A Creative Minds Biography. Minneapolis: Carolrhoda Books, 2004.

Sherman, Josepha. *The Constitution.* A Primary Source Library of American Citizenship. New York: Rosen, 2004.

BIBLIOGRAPHY

Bowen, Catherine Drinker. *Miracle at Philadelphia: The Story of the Constitutional Convention, May to September 1787.* Boston: Little, Brown, 1966.

Farrand, Max, editor. *The Records of the Federal Convention of 1787.* New Haven: Yale University Press, 1966.

Fleming, Thomas. *Liberty! The American Revolution.* New York: Viking, 1997.

Hamilton, Alexander, James Madison, and John Jay. *The Federalist Papers.* New York: New American Library, 1961.

INDEX